POVERTY
OF
SPIRIT

by
Johannes Baptist Metz

Translated by
John Drury
Inclusive Language Version by
Carole Farris

PAULIST PRESS
New York/Mahwah, N.J.

A Paulist Press Edition, originally published under the title *Armut im geiste* by Verlag Ars Sacra Josef Müller, Munich, W. Germany. NIHIL OBSTAT: Rev. Robert E. Hunt, S.T.D., *Censor Librorum,* IMPRIMATUR: ✠ Thomas A. Boland, S.T.D., *Archbishop of Newark,* March 19, 1968.

Library of Congress Cataloging-in-Publication Data

Metz, Johannes Baptist, 1928–
    [Armut im Geiste. English]
    Poverty of spirit / by Johannes Baptist Metz : translated by John Drury ; inclusive language version by Carole Farris.—Rev. ed.
       p. cm.
    ISBN 0-8091-3799-2 (alk. paper)
    1. Poverty—Religious aspects—Christianity. 2. Spiritual life—Catholic Church. 3. Catholic Church—Doctrines. I. Title.
BV4647.P6M4313   1998
241′.4—dc21   97-49919
                                                     CIP

Published by Paulist Press
997 Macarthur Boulevard
Mahwah, New Jersey 07430

Printed and bound in the
United States of America

Contents

Foreword

Becoming a human being involves more than conception and birth. It is a mandate and a mission, a command and a decision. We each have an open-ended relationship to ourselves. We do not possess our being unchallenged; we cannot take our being for granted as God does. Nor do we possess it in the same way as other creatures around us. Other animals, for example, survive in mute innocence and cramped necessity. With no future horizons, they are what they are from the start; the law of their life and being is spelled out for them, and they resign themselves to these limits without question.

We, however, are challenged and questioned from the depths of our boundless spirit. Being is entrusted to us as a summons, which we are each to accept and consciously acknowledge. We are never simply a being that is "there" and "ready-made," just for the asking. From the very start we are something that can Be, a being who must win selfhood and decide what it is to be. We must fully *become* what we *are*—a human being. To become human through the exercise of our freedom—that is the law of our Being.

Now this freedom, which leaves us to ourselves, is not pure arbitrariness or unchecked whim; it is not devoid of law and necessity. It reveals itself at work when we accept and approve with all our heart the being that is committed to us, when we make it so much our own that it seems to be our idea from the first. The inescapable "truth" of our Being is such that it makes our freedom possible rather than threatening it (cf. Jn. 8:32). Thus the free process of becoming a human being unfolds as a process of service. In biblical terms it is "obedience" (cf. Phil. 2:8) and faithfulness to the humanity entrusted to us.

However, this process of freely becoming human has its own inherent temptation. By its very nature this process is a trial; imbedded in it is the danger of going awry. Entrusted with the task of making ourselves human, we face danger at every side. We are always a potential rebel. We can secretly betray the humanity entrusted to us, and we have done precisely this from the very beginning (the first human beings refused to embrace the Being entrusted to them). We can try to run away from ourselves, from the burdens and difficulties of our lot, even going so far as to take our own life. Under the myriad evasions of a materialistic Docetism, we can "stifle" the truth of our Being (cf. Rom. 1:18). In short, we can fail to obey this truth, thus aborting the work of becoming a human being.

On the other hand, we may withstand this temptation and lovingly accept the truth of our Being. For the moment we shall call this attitude "love of self." Here we might glimpse the deep and positive significance of an attitude whose ethical and religious scope is usually overlooked and underrated, even when we use the eyes of faith. Understood correctly, our love for ourselves, our "yes" to our self, may be regarded as the "categorical imperative" of the Christian faith: You shall lovingly accept the humanity entrusted to you! You shall be obedient to your destiny! You shall not continually try to escape it! You shall be true to yourself! You shall embrace yourself!

Our self-acceptance is the basis of the Christian creed. Assent to God starts in our sincere assent to ourselves, just as sinful flight from God starts in our flight from ourselves. In accepting the chalice of our existence, we show our obedience to the will of the Creator in heaven (cf. Mt. 26:39–42); in rejecting it, we reject God. Knowing the temptation that humanity itself is, knowing how readily we try to escape the harsh distress of the human situation, knowing how difficult it is for us to bear with ourselves and how quickly we feel betrayed by ourselves, knowing how difficult it is for us not to hate ourselves (as Bernanos points out), we can then understand why God had to prescribe "self-love" as a virtue and one of the great commandments. We can then understand why we constantly need the help of God's grace. We can then realize how much easier it is to say "no" instead of "yes" to oneself, and why all asceticism is first designed to serve this great "yes."

We must learn to accept ourselves in the painful experiment of living. We must embrace the spiritual adventure of becoming human, moving through the many stages that lie between birth and death. Even the life of the child is darkened by the repulsive enigma of death. Soon enough, with our first feeble explorations into the uncharted inner depths of our personalities, are we tempted to an outright denial of what is most our own. Our flight from ourselves begins early.

God "became human" and took on our flesh. We say this all too casually, because inadvertently we are accustomed to consider only the biological event, the external process. But the assumption of a human's type of Being is primarily a spiritual venture pulsing through the free activity of our heart. It is an unfolding story, an inner journey; it commences with conception and birth, but these events do not tell the whole story.

God becomes human: What are the spiritual lineaments of this process? What does it involve? What motivations lie behind it? Paul describes it in a famous passage (Phil. 2:5-11). The Synoptics also have something to say about it, describing its inner thrust in the story of Jesus' temptation in the desert. Unless we are greatly mistaken, this story is the biblical way of presenting the spiritual process involved in God's assumption of humanity.

God Becomes Human

Then Jesus was led up by the Spirit into the wilderness to be tempted by the devil. And he fasted forty days and forty nights, and afterward he was hungry. And the tempter came and said to him, "If you are the Begotten One, command these stones to become loaves of bread." But he answered, "It is written, 'One shall not live by bread alone, but by every word that proceeds from the mouth of God'" [Deut. 8:3].

Then the devil took him to the holy city, and set him on the pinnacle of the temple, and said to him, "If you are the Only Begotten One, throw yourself down; for it is written, 'God will give the angels charge of you,' and 'On their hands they will bear you up, lest you strike your foot against a stone'" [Ps. 90:11-12].

Jesus said to Satan, "Again it is written, 'You shall not tempt the Lord your God'" [Deut. 6:16].

Again the devil took him to a very high mountain, and showed him all the kingdoms of the world and the glory of them; and Satan said to him, "All these I will give you, if you will fall down and worship me." Then Jesus said to the devil, "Begone, Satan! for it is written, 'You shall worship the Lord your God and God only shall you serve'" [Deut. 6:13].

Then the devil left him, and behold, angels came and ministered to him (Mt. 4:1-11).

Let us overlook the external process involved in these temptations; let us try to focus on their underlying intention, on the basic strategy at work. We can then say that the three temptations represent three assaults on the "poverty" of Jesus, on the self-renunciation through that he chose to redeem us. They represent an assault on the radical and uncompromising step he has taken: to come down from God and become human.

To become human means to become "poor," to have nothing that one might brag about before God. To become human means to have no support and no power, save the enthusiasm and commitment of one's own heart. Becoming human involves proclaiming the poverty of the human spirit in the face of the total claims of a transcendent God.

With the courageous acceptance of such poverty, the divine epic of our salvation began. Jesus held back nothing; he clung to nothing, and nothing served as a shield for him. Even his true origin did not shield him: "He....did not count equality with God a thing to be grasped, but emptied himself" (Phil. 2:6).

Satan, however, tries to obstruct this self-renunciation, this thoroughgoing "poverty." Satan wants to make Jesus strong, for what the devil really fears is the powerlessness of God in the humanity Christ has assumed. Satan fears the trojan horse of an open human heart that will remain true to its native poverty, suffer the misery and abandonment that is humanity's, and thus save humankind. Satan's temptation is an assault on God's self-renunciation, an enticement to strength, security and spiritual abundance; for these things will obstruct God's saving approach to humanity in the dark robes of frailty and weakness.

Satan tries to appeal to the divinity in Jesus, tempered with the gravity and grandeur of his humanity. As a matter of fact, Satan always tries to stress the spiritual strength of human beings and our divine character and has done this from the beginning. "You will be like God": that is Satan's slogan. It is *the* temptation the Evil One has set before us in countless variations, urging us to reject the truth about the humanity we have been given.

Satan joins hands with Docetism and Monophysitism, wanting God to remain simply God. Satan wants the Incarnation to be an empty show, where God dresses up in human costume but doesn't really commit totally to the role. The devil wants to make the Incarnation a piece of mythology, a divine puppet show. That is the strategy for making sure that the earth remains exclusively Satan's—and humankind, too. Even before we really woke up to our freedom, Satan began the assault, wooing us with soft words or confusing us with a web of deceit. As a result we were never impartially summoned to personal decision.

"You're hungry," Satan tells Jesus. "You need be hungry no longer. You can change all that with a miracle. You stand trembling on a pinnacle, overlooking a dark abyss. You need no longer put up with this frightening experience, this dangerous plight; you can command the angels to protect you from falling...." Satan's temptation calls upon Jesus to remain strong like God, to stand within a protecting circle of angels, to hang on to his divinity (Phil. 2:6). The Evil One urges him to flee from the desert (the prototype of our abject poverty), to sneak away from our miserable lot that cries out to heaven. For hunger becomes a human hunger only when it can never be fully allayed; desire becomes a human desire only when it can remain unfulfilled. And nearness to the abyss becomes a human experience only when one can no longer call upon helping hands for protection.

Thus the temptation in the desert would have Jesus betray humanity in the name of God (or, diabolically, God in the name of humanity). Jesus' "no" to Satan is his "yes" to our poverty. He did not cling to his divinity. He did not simply dip into our existence, wave a magic wand of divine life over us and then hurriedly retreat to his eternal home. Nor did he leave us with a tattered dream, letting us brood over the mystery of our existence.

Instead, Jesus subjected himself to our plight. He immersed himself in our misery and followed our road to the end. He did not escape from the torment of our life, nobly repudiating humanity. With the full weight of his divinity he descended into the abyss of human existence, penetrating its darkest depths. He was not spared from the dark mystery of our poverty as human beings.

Here was a person who was "tempted as we are, yet without sinning" (Heb. 4:15). And sin does not heighten the saga or the suffering of our uncertain plight; instead, it compromises and mitigates them. Enmeshed in sin, we do not drink in our poverty down to the last drop; we do not stare it full in the face. By sinning we make a secret compromise with the offspring of sin—the forces of suffering and death; we join forces with them before they can assault us and make us truly poor.

Christ, the sinless one, experienced the poverty of human existence more deeply and more excruciatingly than any other person could. He saw its many faces, including those shadowy aspects we never glimpse. In the poverty of his passion, he had no consolation, no companion angels, no guiding star, no Abba in heaven. All he had was his own lonely heart, bravely facing its ordeal even as far as the cross (Phil. 2:8).

Have we really understood the impoverishment that Christ endured? Everything was taken from him during the passion, even the love that drove him to the cross. No longer did he savor his own love, no longer did he feel any spark of enthusiasm. His heart gave out and a feeling of utter helplessness came over him. Truly he emptied himself (Phil. 2:7). God's merciful hand no longer sustained him. God's countenance was hidden during the passion, and Christ gaped into the darkness of nothingness and abandonment where God was no longer present. He reached his destiny, stretched taut between a despising earth that had rejected him and a faceless heaven thundering God's "no" to sinful humankind. Jesus paid the price of futility. He became utterly poor.

In this total renunciation, however, Jesus perfected and proclaimed in action what took place in the depths of his being: he professed and accepted our humanity, he took on and endured our lot, he stepped down from his divinity. He came to us where we really are—with all our broken dreams and lost hopes, with the meaning of existence slipping through our fingers. He came and stood with us, struggling with his whole heart to have us say "yes" to our innate poverty.

God's fidelity to us is what gives us the courage to be true to ourselves. And the legacy of God's total commitment to humankind, the proof of God's fidelity to our poverty, is the cross. The cross is the sacrament of poverty of spirit, the sacrament of authentic humanness in a sinful world. It is the sign that one human being remained true to his own humanity, that he accepted it in full obedience.

Hanging in utter weakness on the cross, Christ revealed the divine meaning of our Being. It said something for the Jews and pagans that they found the cross scandalous and foolish (1 Cor. 1:23). To the enlightened humanitarians and liberals of a later day the cross provokes only flat irony or weary skepticism. These self-styled advocates of humanity are more experienced; they are too indifferent to find the cross scandalous, yet not so naive as to laugh at its foolishness. And what is it to us? Well, no one is exempted from the poverty of the cross; there is no guarantee against its intrusion. The antipathy to it found its way into the very midst of Christ's disciples: "You will all fall away because of me this night" (Mt. 26:31).

Judas' betrayal may have been the result of frenzied impatience with Jesus' poverty, or a futile attempt to pressure Jesus into using his divine resources instead of accepting human impotence. In any case, it is not an isolated instance. Poverty of spirit is always betrayed most by those who are closest to it. It is the disciples of Christ in the Church who criticize and subvert it most savagely.

Perhaps that is why Jesus related the parable of the wheat grain. Finding in it a lesson for himself, he passed it on to his Church, so that it might be remembered down through the ages, especially when the poverty intrinsic to human existence became repugnant: "Unless a grain of wheat falls into the earth and dies, it remains alone; but if it dies, it bears much fruit" (Jn. 12:24).

We Become Human

"Have this mind among yourselves, which was in Christ Jesus: who, though he was in the form of God, did not count equality with God a thing to be grasped, but emptied himself, taking the form of a servant, being born in the likeness of humans. And being found in human form, he humbled himself and became obedient unto death, even death on the cross" (Phil. 2:5-8).

The Synoptics summed up this attitude in the phrase "poverty of spirit" (Mt. 5:3). In their accounts of Jesus' temptation, it is depicted as obedient acceptance of our natural impoverishment, which culminates in forlorn death on the cross: "Though he was rich, yet for your sake he became poor" (2 Cor. 8:9).

Christ showed us how to really become human beings. In him we see the unimagined heights and depths of our human lot. He is the prototype of human existence, the "first-born of all creation" (Col. 1:15), the "son of earth." In him we find out what it means to be human; in him we find the kernel and the acme of our existence.

We cannot say that we had any right to the divine work of reunification (cf. Eph. 1:10) that was accomplished through Christ. Rather we are at once so needy and yet noble that we discover ourselves, with our deepest and most intense potentialities, not by deducing the latter from a static notion of human nature, but by seeing them reflected in the free, gratuitous action of God on our behalf. God did not reject us or stay aloof from us, rather he treated us with self-sacrificing love. In giving us the Only Begotten One, God showed us what our existence is, showed us the true nature of our humanness, and showed us the proper spirit to have in becoming a human being: the spirit of poverty.

The significance of this spirit for us can also be seen from another angle: God does not undermine our humanity, but protects and insures it. God's truth makes us free (cf. Jn. 8:32). Unlike the pagan gods, God does not expropriate our humanity. In drawing us to the Divine self, God sets us free. God is the guardian of our humanity, who lets us be what we are. When God draws the creature near, the creature becomes all the more important. When God draws near, the glow of our humanity shines even more brightly before us. God brightens our true greatness as human beings. Because of the divine transcendence, the world and we do not wither away in God's presence but assume our own proper value.

God has come to us in grace. We have been endowed with God's life and our life made God's. In doing this, God did not mitigate or eliminate our innate poverty, but actually intensified it and outdid it. God's grace does not cause estrangement and excess, as sin does. It reveals the full depths of our destiny (resulting from God's salvific initiative in history), which we could not have imagined by ourselves.

A human being with grace is a human being who has been emptied, who stands impoverished before God, who has nothing of which to boast: "For God is at work in you, both to will and to work for God's good pleasure" (Phil. 2:13). This person works out her or his salvation in the poverty of "fear and trembling" (Phil. 2:12). Grace does not erase our poverty; it transforms it totally, allowing it to share in the poverty of Jesus' own immolated heart (cf. Rom. 8:17).

This poverty, then, is not just another virtue, one among many. It is a necessary ingredient in any authentic Christian attitude toward life. Without it there can be no Christianity and no imitation of Christ. It is no accident that "poverty of spirit" is the first of the beatitudes. What is the sorrow of those who mourn, the suffering of the persecuted, the self-forgetfulness of the merciful, or the humility of the peacemakers—what are these if not variations of spiritual poverty? This spirit is also the mother of the three-fold mystery of faith, hope and charity. It is the doorway through which we must pass to become authentic human beings. Only through poverty of spirit do we draw near to God; only through it does God draw near to us. Poverty of spirit is the meeting point of heaven and earth, the mysterious place where God and humanity encounter each other, the point where infinite mystery meets concrete existence.

The Innate Poverty of Humanity

When we encounter Jesus Christ, we become sharply aware of our innate poverty as human beings. We see then the dire want of a person who lives on the bread of eternity, whose food is to do the will of God (cf. Jn. 4:54). Did not Jesus live in continual dependence on someone else? Was not his very existence hidden in the mysterious will of his Abba? Was he not so thoroughly poor that he had to go begging for his very personality from the transcendent utterance of the Abba? Was not his whole life buried in the mysterious will of his Abba?

We are all beggars. We are all members of a species that is not sufficient unto itself. We are all creatures plagued by unending doubts and restless, unsatisfied hearts. Of all creatures, we are the poorest and the most incomplete. Our needs are always beyond our capacities, and we only find ourselves when we lose ourselves.

We cannot rest content in ourselves. In the elements and experiences of our life, to which we give meaning, we do not find satisfying light and protective security. We only find these things in the intangible mystery that overshadows our heart from the first day of our lives, awakening questions and wonderment and luring us beyond ourselves. We surrender ourselves to this mystery, as a person in love surrenders to the mystery of the beloved and there finds rest. We are creatures whose being is sheltered and protected only insofar as we open ourselves up to intangible, greater realities. We are at peace in the open, unconquered precincts of mystery.

If we leave our dreamy conceptions aside and focus on our naked poverty, when the mask falls and the core of our Being is revealed, it soon becomes obvious that we are religious "by nature," that religion is the secret dowry of our Being. In the midst of our existence there unfolds the bond *(re-ligio)* that ties us to the infinitely transcendent mystery of God, the insatiable interest in the Absolute that captivates us and underlines our poverty.

At the core of our existence, a "transcendental neediness" holds sway. It spurs and supports all our longings and desires, works itself out through them, but is never exhausted by them. When they are fulfilled it ruthlessly exposes how provisional they were. It condemns us to a restless pilgrimage through the universe in search of a final satisfaction, an "Amen," which the poor know is theirs only in "the kingdom of heaven" (cf. Mt. 5:3).

The unending nature of our poverty as human beings is our only innate treasure. We are unlimited indigence since our very self-possession, the integrity and lucidity of our coming-to-Being, spring not from ourselves but from the intangible mystery of God. The ultimate meaning of being human is hidden in God. A human being is the *ecstatic appearance of Being,* and becoming fully human is an ever growing appropriation of this ecstasis of Being. This demands an attentive receptivity and obedient assent to the total claim and inescapable quandary that the mystery of God poses to our human existence.

Although we do not choose to be religious or non-religious in regard to our innermost Being, nonetheless we are faced with the choice implied in self-acceptance or self-alienation. We can surrender to the ecstatic poverty of our Being, through "poverty of spirit" abiding in it. This acceptance can reach the heights of mysticism, where through grace the human spirit overtakes its innate ecstasis and becomes one with it. But we can also dissemble our dependence on God, close in upon ourselves, "take scandal" at our innate poverty. The temptation to do this is great. The radical indigence of our humanity has something repulsive about it. It devastates us, tears down self-created defenses and jars us out of the familiar, routine horizon of everyday life.

All too easily, we live alienated from the truth of our Being. The threatening "nothingness" of our poor infinity and infinite poverty drives us hither and thither among the distractions of everyday cares. We run away from the "night," with its fear and trembling before the truth of our Being, into the bright lights of easily understood platitudes. St. Paul termed this as seeking the security of the "Law," a security that distorts the elusive mystery and open authenticity of our Being. The Bible calls "Pharisees" those who try to evade the depth of their innate poverty through clinging to the Law. They are "rich in spirit" and the most dangerous opponents of poverty, and hence of Jesus, because they vaunt their own brand of piety and seek to set up God as an opponent of poverty.

Left to ourselves, we still remain the prisoner of our own Being. We cannot successfully hide for long our mysterious Being. If we attempt this, the truth of our Being haunts us with its nameless emissary: anxiety. This becomes the prophet of the repressed mystery of our Being; with its alienation, anxiety takes the place of the scorned poverty. In the final analysis we have one of two choices: to obediently accept our innate poverty or to become the slave of anxiety.[1]

---

[1] On this theological interpretation of anxiety, see Johannes Metz, *Advent Gottes,* Sammulung Sigma.

The Poverty of Being Human Freely Accepted: Poverty of Spirit

We mentioned earlier that humble acceptance of our authentic Being is self-love in the Christian sense. In biblical terms it is "poverty of spirit." It is we human beings bearing witness to ourselves, professing loyalty to our radical poverty, and shouldering the weight of self-emptying. It is our consent to self-surrender.

In poverty of spirit we learn to accept ourselves as beings who do not belong to ourselves. It is not a virtue that one "acquires"; as such, it could easily turn into a personal possession that would challenge our authentic poverty. We truly "possess" this radical poverty only when we forget ourselves and look the other way. As Jesus put it: "No one who puts a hand to the plow and looks back is fit for the reign of God" (Lk. 9:62). To look back for reassurance is to try to acquire possession and full control over this virtue, which amounts to losing it.

Poverty can never be isolated from the roots of existence and laid hold of. It is thoroughgoing interiority. It is the concentrated commitment of all our capabilities and powers. It cannot be viewed abstractly; it must involve total personal dedication. Like truth, it must be lived (cf. 1 Jn. 1:16) from the depths of our heart, where our existence is unified and where our act of self-acceptance is unified and harmonized with our conscious presence to Being.

The fulfilled ones are the ones who dare to forget themselves and offer up their heart. "The one who loves his or her life loses it, and the one who hates his or her life in this world will keep it for eternal life" (Jn. 12:25). To be able to surrender oneself and become "poor" is, in biblical theology, to be with God, to find one's hidden nature in God; in short, it is "heaven."

To stick to oneself and to serve one's own interests is to be damned; it is "hell." Here we discover, only too late, that the tabernacle of self is empty and barren. For we can only find ourselves and truly love ourselves through the poverty of an immolated heart.

This self-abandonment does not work itself out as some vague mysticism, in which the world and human beings are left behind. It constantly adverts to human beings and their world. God drew near to us as our brother and sister and our neighbor, as "one of these" (cf. Mt. 25:40–45). Our relationship with God is decided in our encounter with other human beings. One of the non-canonical sayings of Jesus is: "The ones who see their neighbor see God."

The only image of God is the face of our neighbor, who is also the sibling of God's First-Born, of God's own likeness (2 Cor. 4:4; Col. 1:15). Our human neighbor now becomes a "sacrament" of God's hidden presence among us, a mediator between God and humanity. Every authentic religious act is directed toward the concreteness of God in our human neighbors and their world. There it finds its living fulfillment and its transcendent point of contact. Could humanity be taken more seriously than that? Is anything more radically anthropocentric than God's creative love?

The nearness of God and the nearness of humans run closely parallel in the Christian outlook, for which the humanity of Christ is the direct manifestation of the eternal Creator (cf. Jn. 8:19; 12:45; 13:5–11). Love of neighbor, then, is not something different from love of God; it is merely the earthly side of the same coin. At their source they are one (cf. Mt. 22:37–40; 1 Jn. 4:7–21): that is the startling and distinctive note in the Christian message.

Hence, it is in our relations with our sisters and brothers that our spirit of poverty is preserved, that our readiness for sacrifice enables us to become truly human. It is in these terms that Scripture describes salvation and damnation. It is as if God had forgotten about God entirely. In the judgment scene, God is visible only in the visage of other human beings. Blessed are they who have served their neighbors and cared for their needs; cursed are they who have selfishly disregarded their brothers and sisters and rejected the light of love and human community. The latter, in trying to enrich and bolster their own selves, have turned their neighbor into the enemy and thus created their own hell.

Poverty of spirit does not bring us from human beings to God by isolating these components into separate little packages: God—me—others. (God can never be just one more reality alongside others.) It operates through the radical depths of human encounter itself. In total self-abandonment and full commitment to another we become completely poor, and the depths of infinite mystery open up to us from within this other person. In this order, we come before God. If we commit ourselves to this person without reservation, if we accept and do not try to use this person as an instrument of self-assertion, our human encounter occurs within the horizon of unending mystery. This openness to others can be enjoyed only in the poverty of self-abandonment; egoism destroys it.

The Concrete Shapes of Poverty

To become human as Christ did is to practice poverty of spirit, to obediently accept our innate poverty as human beings. This acceptance can take place in many of life's circumstances where the very possibility of being human is challenged and open to question. The inevitable summons to surrender to the truth of our Being suggests itself in many ways. Here we want to highlight the most important forms that our poverty takes, to show how our daily experiences point us toward the desert wastes of poverty.

There is the poverty of the average person's life, whose life goes unnoticed by the world. It is the *poverty of the commonplace.* There is nothing heroic about it; it is the poverty of the common lot, devoid of ecstasy.

Jesus was poor in this way. He was no model figure for humanists, no great artist or statesman, no diffident genius. He was a frighteningly simple man, whose only talent was to do good. His one great passion in his life was his "Abba." Yet it was precisely in this way that he demonstrated "the wonder of empty hands" (Bernanos), the great potential of the person on the street, whose radical dependence on God is no different from anyone else's. Such a person has no talent but that of one's own heart, no contribution to make except self-abandonment, no consolation save God alone.

Related to this poverty is the *poverty of misery and neediness.* Jesus was no stranger to this poverty either. He was a beggar, knocking on people's doors. He knew hunger, exile and the loneliness of the outcast (so much that he will judge us on these things: cf. Mt. 25:31–46). He had no place to lay his head (cf. Mt. 8:20), not even in death—except a gibbet on which to stretch his body.

Christ did not "identify" with misery or "choose" it; it was his lot. That is the only way we really taste misery, for it has its own inscrutable laws. His life tells us that such neediness can become a blessed sacrament of "poverty of spirit." With nothing of one's own to provide security, the wretched person has only hope—the virtue so quickly misunderstood by the secure and rich. The latter confuse it with shallow optimism and a childish trust in life, whereas hope emerges in the shattering experience of living "despite all hope" (Rom. 4:18). We really hope when we no longer have anything of our own. Any possession or personal strength tempts us to a vain self-reliance, just as material wealth easily becomes a temptation to "spiritual opulence."

In contrast to the above forms, there is the *poverty of uniqueness and superiority*, which is the honor and burden of the great people in history. They each carried a secret in their hearts that made them great and lonely; each had an exceptional mission, which, because it was without parallel, offered neither protection nor guarantee among other human beings. No one enjoys such responsibility.

Satan attacks this poverty in Jesus, this call to stand alone, deprived of companionship and community. Every secret makes one poor, especially when its enigma scandalizes others and is misunderstood. "Be like the rest of humanity," whispers Satan, "feed on bread, wealth and worldly prestige—like the rest of us." It is a temptation put also to each of us: to renounce the poverty of our unique, mysterious personality, to do just what "everyone else" does. We are encouraged to repress the painful loneliness and individuality that foreshadow the terrible poverty and desolation of death, to betray our mission, whatever its form, be it unswerving loyalty to another person, an undaunted love, the unyielding quest for justice or the lonely call to duty. "Don't rock the boat. Why make a nuisance of yourself? Why not live from the daily bread of compromise? When in Rome do as the Romans—*vox populi, vox Dei!* You'll only be overruled and shouted down, without getting a word of thanks."

So the argument runs, urging everyone to the average, thoughtless mediocrity that is veiled and protected by the legalities, conventions and flattery of a society that craves endorsement for every activity, yet retreats into public anonymity. Indeed, with such anonymity it will risk everything—and nothing!—*except* a genuine, open, personal commitment. Yet without paying the price of poverty implied in such commitments, no one will fulfill her or his mission as a human being. For only poverty enables us to find true selfhood.

Closely related to the poverty of individual uniqueness is the *poverty of our provisional nature as human beings.* This trait is deeply embedded in our existence. As creatures in history we cannot rest in the security of the present. Our life today does not stand still; it stands on the foundation of a long past, to which there is also a long future ahead. A contemporary philosopher remarked how "our origin continues as our future." What the past has made us is yet to come. The mysterious, intangible beginnings of our life become visible only at its end. Only in the throes of death do our childhood dreams find realization. The future is the unfinished destiny of the past.

Thus, to take possession of our past and hold it securely, we must face the risks of a future that is yet to be. Only by taking this risk do we conquer the wellsprings of our life and follow the law of our Being. Our historical present suffers from the poverty of provisionality. This is exemplified in John the Baptist, an image of our provisional existence if there ever was one: "I am not the one....After me comes he who was before me (Jn. 1:20-21, 27). I do not belong to myself; I am a stranger to myself, a destitute land between the past promise and the still to come fulfillment. I have nothing to make me strong or rich. Everything within me strains forward, is set on edge in prophetic anticipation—what poverty a prophet endures!—of an intangible future, and I am certain to find therein my true self, the promised land of my loving God."

We are only too ready to hide the poverty and neediness of our existence in history. We do not like the risks faced by the prophet, the dire poverty of hope, the life of a person who finds support in the intangible promise of a provisional present.

Jesus described this mentality when he spoke of those whose time "is always here" (Jn. 7:6). For these persons the present is something they can lay hands on, the past is the familiar strain of custom running through the present, and the future is something carefully plotted out *in the present.* They are shocked by the inadequacy and uncertainty of historical existence with its unanswered questions and desires. So they exclude this open dimension of existence from the horizon of their understanding and performance. They accuse the forerunner and prophet of being "the enemy of tradition," of idolizing the passing moment and so disregarding the past, the custodian of which they pride themselves on being. They have no sympathy for the poverty and martyrdom involved in human incompleteness and humankind's provisional nature.

The prophets of a future promise are spurned and misunderstood. "Serve the law that has been handed down to us," say the people around them. In fact, they do remain true to the law of our historical heritage. In them the continuity of history is maintained. In their poverty and effacement, the threads of history are woven together and the truth of history emerges. They sustain the priceless secret of humanity for us, rescuing it from the sterile routine and illusory self-evidence of the habitual. Their powerful witness challenges us out of a hardened, unquestioning acceptance of the present into the poverty of the provisional future. As pioneers and pacesetters, they come to us under many different guises—teacher, philosopher, statesperson, doctor, writer, priest, etc. They move closer to the mystery of our heritage, plunge into it and let it close over them.

What about those who reject humanity's provisionality? They will betray the wellsprings of their past heritage and sever themselves from it. They will deafen themselves to the call and challenge of the present. Moreover, because all historical understanding bears a prophetic character, understanding the present demands of us that we be in advance of it, that the range of our vision reach out into that distance where the horizon and frontier-line of the present is drawn. To use the legacy of the past as a means of self-aggrandizement is to succumb to mythology. So, such people isolate themselves from the power of their legacy and choose to operate within the boundaries of a transparent and manageable present. When set before the rather gaunt visage of a life that thrives on the mystery and complexity of history, this form of existence seems, at first, so much richer and "come of age."

This was the spirit that the Pharisees cultivated among the Israelites. They used the past to bolster and support their own righteousness; the promise made to Abraham became a piece of mythology. Only John the Baptist recalled them to their original heritage (cf. Eph. 1:4). To become fully human in history, one must succumb to the poverty of our provisional nature. This holds for humankind in its entirety and for each and every individual as well.

Our existence in history is marked by another form of poverty as well: the *poverty of finiteness.* Through the transcendental expanse of our spirits we live in the open air, in the future of unlimited potentialities. Our task is not to lose ourselves there, but to make something of ourselves through them. We make them our potentialities by a historically unique and irrevocable personal decision, through which we find a foothold in the thrust of our existence.

This very decision, however, reveals the poverty of our existence. For it involves the sacrifice and surrender of a thousand other possibilities. Our decision is effective only when we accept this risk of human poverty; otherwise, we must fall prey to ceaseless experimentation.

The poverty of finiteness is also experienced in another way. The moment of decision is not always open to us, nor always repeatable. There is an element of finality about it. There is a moment (cf. Col. 4:5; Eph. 5:16), an hour (Jn. 2:4) when opportunity knocks, when we can integrate the elements of our life and make them whole. By the same token, we may miss our hour, for it is not an ever-present one (cf. Jn. 7:6-8) that we can, consequently, manage as we will. Even our special moment reveals our impoverished finiteness.

Poverty has many other visages in our life. Every stirring of genuine *love* makes us poor. It dominates the whole human person, makes absolute claims upon us (cf. Mt. 22:37), and thus subverts all extra-human assurances of security. The true lover must be unprotected and give of himself or herself without reservation or question; and must display lifelong fidelity.

Every *genuine human encounter* must be inspired by poverty of spirit. We must forget ourselves in order to let the other person approach us. We must be able to open up to the other person, to let that person's distinctive personality unfold—even though it often frightens or repels us. We often keep the other person down, and only see what we want to see; thus we never really encounter the mysterious secret of their being, only ourselves. Failing to risk the poverty of encounter, we indulge in a new form of self-assertion and pay a price for it: loneliness. Because we did not risk the poverty of openness (cf. Mt. 10:39), our lives are not graced with the warm fullness of human existence. We are left with only a shadow of our real self.

Finally, there is the inescapable *poverty of death.* It is the lodestone for all the various forms of poverty of spirit: the cutting loneliness of our own Being, the lonely resolve of loyalty, the apparent futility of our love, along with the other manifestations of poverty. All these others are merely the prelude and the testing ground for the critical moment of death. It is here that the truth of our being is judged irrevocably. In death we experience the great poverty of our human nature; in death we carry out our obedience to our human destiny, with all its uncertainty and critical decisiveness.

Death reveals the self-annihilating quality of poverty in all its fullness. We slip away from ourselves entirely. Our freely fashioned destiny is concealed and taken out of our grasp. In the obedient and suffering acceptance of these depths of powerlessness, we are left with only the power of self-abandonment. At this point poverty comes to full achievement. Its meaning comes to full clarity in the cry of Jesus on the Cross: "Abba, into your hands I commit my Spirit" (Lk. 23:46). Sub-mission to the forces of one's own death-bound nature becomes obedient self-abandonment to the Abba, a total commitment to the full power of faith, hope and love. In abandoning ourselves to poverty, we abandon ourselves to God—whether we consciously realize it or not. Poverty of spirit becomes the doorway to an encounter with God and to immersion in transcendence.

Thus poverty of spirit is not just one virtue among many. It is the hidden component of every transcending act, the ground of every "theological virtue." Our infinite poverty is the shadow-image of God's inner infinity; in it, thanks to God's grace and mercy, we are able to find our full existence. We discover in its unremitting demands upon us the unmistakable interpretation of God's will. It is no arbitrary will that sweeps across our being without appeal to our freedom. It is within our very being that the claims of this will find their lettering. That is why the individual guises of this poverty are the possibilities bestowed on us by God, the opportunities enabling us to become real human beings. They are the chalice that God holds out to us; if we drink it, we allow God's holy will to work on us.

To be sure, none of us drinks the chalice of our existence to the last drop. None of us is fully obedient. Each of us falls short of the human nature entrusted to us. We are all compromised in our acknowledgment of the truth of our being and in our work of becoming human (since that original fault at the dawn of humankind). We never fully grasp the image of our impoverished being. There is a rift between ideal and actual life, between the real thrust of our life and our actual life from day to day. We always remain a promise never quite fulfilled, an image only dimly seen through a mirror (1 Cor. 13:9–12). We always stand at "a distance from our own selves, never fully sounding the depths of that being called 'I.'"

Our eyes and heart give way before we experience the full poverty of death. We are mercifully spared from the ultimate horror. Only dimly aware of it all, we stride across the range of our destiny. We never plumb the full depths of our poverty because, even in the attempt to accept and take it upon ourselves, we encounter our powerlessness. We are, to use the relevant theological term, concupiscent. Concupiscence—this is what measures the meagerness of our poverty.

Because of our concupiscence, we cannot experience our impotence to the fullest. In contrast to the Chosen One, we do not experience the full passion of our existence and the bitter truth of our poverty. It is our "happy fault."

This ancestral refusal to face our lot is a standing temptation for us. It leads us to give way to the same attitude in our *free* choices and to reject the humanity we have been endowed with. This freely chosen refusal is the root of all human guilt, the acute temptation faced by humankind.

The Dregs of Poverty: Worship

All the great experiences of life—freedom, encounter, love, death—are worked out in the silent turbulence of an impoverished spirit. A gentleness comes over us when we confront such decisive moments. We are quietly but deeply moved by a mature encounter; we become suddenly humble when we are overtaken by love. A certain luster plays over the visage of a dying person.

As we draw near to our real wellsprings, our thoughts become devout, our understanding mellows, and our words slacken. Our judgment becomes reserved and our objectivity becomes reverent. Philosophy then becomes open and receptive, readily accepting and shouldering the poverty and uncertainty of our spirit. How can we explain the rise within our hearts and spirits of this wordless, empty, but deeply stirring piety? Why this withdrawal from the teeming marketplace of facile thoughts and racy interests into this recollecting poverty of a deep, chilling stillness that invades every recess of our Being?

The reason is that in such experiences the moment of truth arrives (Jn. 2:4); our life and our being are revealed to us. We then glimpse the ground of our existence; we then gaze into the precipitous depths opened up by such experiences. At such moments we are brought, not only in "thought," but in the totality of our Being, before the great mystery that touches the roots of our existence and encircles our spirit even before it is brought home to us with full force.

At such moments we begin to realize that we are accosted and laid hold of even before we lay hold of ourselves. We dimly begin to realize that we are poor, that our power and strength are derived from the wellsprings of invisible mystery.

With faith our fear and trembling find their voice once again. With faith we turn to worship. But our speech is now composed of bold words, "God" and "Abba," and fed by the consoling mystery uttered by Christ: "No one comes to the Abba, but by me" (Jn. 14:6). Worshipping in "spirit and truth" (Jn. 4:23), we no longer bear ourselves with the swagger of the executive who knows what is up and has all under control. We realize now that we are quite under the hand of Another, claimed and summoned to service. We are mistaken, however, if we expect to find in prayer a shelter from the overwhelming force of mystery. It is precisely in prayer that we will cease to perceive this mystery as the distant horizon of our acutely developed human sensitivity and begin to hear about ourselves in its encompassing challenge and summons. Mystery acquires in prayer an identity, a name. What manifested itself as an anonymous presence in the deep stirrings of human emotion reveals itself in prayer as "Emmanuel," as the presence of God with us. So identified, this mystery gains a total power over the full sweep of our human existence. Over the hidden depths and transcending breadth of our spirit? Yes. But that is not the limit of God's power over us. Under a variety of names God is familiar here even to those who reject God outright. In the person who prays, the range of God's power runs from the depths to the surface, right into the course of everyday thoughts and decisions, words and actions.

We no longer have anything that would stand aloof from the imperious appeal of this mystery, no credentials of independence. In worship we hand over even our poverty and pledge it to this mystery of God's all-encompassing presence. Human language achieves its deepest meaning when we, standing before this mystery, utter not the call of retreat from it, but of advance into it; when our word expresses, not alienation from this mystery, but an affirmation of it and a growing commitment of self to it.

Only prayer reveals the precipitous depths of our poverty. Submission to it involves an awareness of someone else. We are so poor that even our poverty is not our own; it belongs to the mystery of God. In prayer we drink the dregs of our poverty, professing the richness and grandeur of someone else: God. The ultimate word of impoverished humankind is: "Not I, but Thou." Only when we commit ourselves without reserve to the recognition of this "Thou" do we hear ourselves endlessly called to the full, taking possession of that priceless, irreplaceable "I" whom we are each meant to be. In the great hours of a person's life this "I" announces itself, not as an achieved reality, but as the possibility we are endlessly called to realize. It is when we, in the poverty of our worshipping spirit, tread before the face of God's freedom, into the mystery of that impenetrable "Thou"—it is then that we find access to the depths of our own Being and worth. Then we really become fully human. In worshipping God we are brought totally before ourselves and to ourselves. This is the case since we are, after all, given to ourselves, called and gathered into the depths of our personal Being, by the address and appeal of God.

Thus prayer is the ultimate realization of humanity. Surrendering everything, even our poverty, we become truly rich: "For when I am weak, then I am strong" (2 Cor. 12:10).